GUMSHOE

Gumshoe

Wendy Morton

To Jodene,
for dreams.
Love,
Wendy
March 24,
2013

Black Moss Press
2007

Library and Archives Canada Cataloguing in Publication

Morton, Wendy, 1940-
Gumshoe / Wendy Morton.
Poems.
ISBN 978-0-88753-434-8
I. Title.
PS8576.O778G84 2007 C811'.6 C2007-904120-5

Cover photo: Tara Walton
Author photo: Rod Punnett
Design: Karen Veryle Monck

Black Moss Press is published at 2450 Byng Road, Windsor, Ontario, Canada N8W3E8. Black Moss books are distributed in Canada and the U.S. by LitDistco. All orders should be directed there.

Black Moss can be contacted on its website at www.blackmosspress.com.

Black Moss acknowledges the generous support for its publishing program from The Canada Council for the Arts and The Ontario Arts Council.

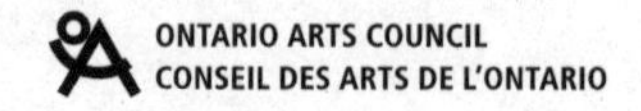

EPIGRAPH

The wonder of the world,
the beauty and the power,
the shapes of things, their colours
lights and shades,
these I saw.
Look ye also
while life lasts.

Graveyard inscription, Cumberland, England

Contents

GLORY

Crows in the dumpster.
Morning. The harbour
still.
One disgruntled seagull.
All that flapping.

GETTING MANURE

You charged the battery
While I was in the Kootenays
investigating the drug king of Kaslo
who lived at the end of graveyard road
or while I was watching the snow fall
on the Japanese Memorial Garden
in New Denver.

"Herman's on his last legs,"
you said in the spring,
meaning the old green Ford,
rusting in place in the woods out back.

You had traveled mid-day
to the neighbour's pile,
loaded Herman until
the tires were near collapse
and hightailed it home
before any cop could see you.

“A gift,” you said, when I came home.
Today, I took a bucket of dark tea
from the manure pile
to the raspberry patch.
Flung it over the ground
in a benediction
to your gifts,
to all that is madcap and dangerous,
to memory, to graveyards,
to raspberries, batteries.

IF I HAD A NAME LIKE ROSIE FERNANDEZ

I would wear gardenias and orchids
in my hair.
I would buy some hot sauce
called " Jump up and kiss me".
I would offer it to strangers.
If I had a name like Rosie Fernandez
I would know how to tango,
I would sing anywhere,
I would tap dance on sidewalks.
I would fall in love insistently,
spend hours in cafes
with a broken heart
and good coffee.

Oh, if I had a name like Rosie Fernandez,
I would know it.

IMPROVISATION

Of course, you improvise, imagine
just for a moment that you
are the person you say you are.
Invent a new name, get a hat.

Or, if you are getting a green tea facial
in Salmon Arm, you can imagine
just for that moment
that it is neither China nor winter.

And the name you have chosen,
just for that moment
means something impressive,
even biblical. Like Rebecca.

But you have entirely forgotten
who she is. Except the name of a movie
you have also forgotten.
You recall someone died.

In a boat. You imagine
there was a cabin. Romance.
Bits of black and white dialogue.
Improvisation. Hats. Death.

LOVE ISN'T

thunder and cinnamon.
Is walls the colour of Provence;
seagulls framed in the skylight,
between clouds and the morning moon;
hoya trailing night perfume;
a level floor;
a new sink;
your hands.

ROSES

You like to tell the story
of how it was, the first time,
when I fell asleep in your arms
in the green chair.
Or how I leaned against you
when I read you poems. Leaned
into you, as I tell it.
And later, you arrived
at the door for the first time
in a tweed sport coat
and green tie, carrying a bouquet.
Was it roses? Roses?

CALL IT

wanting to dance with Neruda,
like the waltz
in the Cartier- Bresson photograph
all black and white swirl
of silk and perfume.
Call it the foxtrot,
the two step, the cha-cha.
Oh, call it the fandango.
Call it the unsweetened,
dark, white, bitter.
Call it the majorette's costume
left at the station.
Call it larkspur, roses, hello.
Call it the garden of rust on bridges,
heartbreak, rattlesnake,
blizzard, sorrow.
Call it hummingbird, heron,
raven, gull. Call it
fogline. Salt.
Love.

THE ANGEL OF THE APPLE TREES

The angel of the apple trees
sings in the branches
of the old tree that shivers
toward the harbour.
It's November. The apples
hang like last year's forgotten
Christmas ornaments.
The angel moves her wings.
The apples drop.
The geese celebrate.
Eat.

AT MOONKEY GROCERIES, VICTORIA

In Chinatown, cherry blossoms line
Fan Tan Alley,
fall into the boxes of fragrant pears,
baby bok choi;
decorate the mangos and starfruit.
Water chestnuts and watercress
are in their element.
Here, in the rain,
spring falls pink.
Opulent.

SQUASH

I want to consider the squash
That grew this summer
in the unexpected garden.
The pumpkins we hadn't planted
sprang between the broccoli plants
and the long green squash
that we couldn't name
that grew between
the spinach and the chard

or what we thought was pumpkin,
but wasn't, that
trailed over the grass
in search of itself.

I want to consider the delicata,
which we planted with expectations,
which grew even
when the water ran out;
and, prolific in sunlight,
like small striped suns
they grew.

I want to consider the meals of squash:
steamed with butter
or baked or mashed.

I want to consider
the custard of pumpkin,
the sun made sun again.

And the long green squash,
of a spring paleness inside
and the exotic almost-pumpkin,
oh, most delicious.

I want to consider the squash,
its surprise, its trespass.
The joy of it,
the shape of it,
the shelves of it,
the great exhalted suns of it.

SMALL PARACHUTES OF LIGHT

If you are still long enough,
the world arrives at your door.
One afternoon, a moth landed at my feet;
a perfect blend of shell and cold ember.
I moved a cedar bough
to mark it on the ground,
to remember where it lay.
I moved my shadow to give light,
and watched it move its wings
and fly away.

If you are still long enough,
the world arrives at your door.
On the beach, I found a single nail
patinated by the sea,
encased in wood. Part of a boat,
I thought, built by a man who loved
silence, who hummed,
who spent mornings on the harbour
listening to the sound of shells
on the tide.

If you are still long enough,
the world arrives at your door.
This winter the jasmine
that had bloomed
for years on the front porch,
put out seed pods that seemed ungainly,
entirely out of place.
I picked them off,
put them on a blue plate
in the kitchen.
One day, toward spring,
the pods broke open,
a hundred seeds,
small parachutes of light
spilled into the air:
a world, arriving.

PLASTINATED: A TRIPTYCH

JUDE

I like this skateboarder,
his gluteus muscles pulled back.
He's a plastic cadaver,
caught in the moment
of his last joy,
all his fluids replaced.

His arms are in flight,
all art and alarm:
he's wearing a red ballcap,
backwards, a black hoodie,
half a pair of jeans,
Nike runners.

We're both smiling.

DANIELLE

is in pirouette
dressed for Swan Lake
in white tutu,
feathered head piece.

Her hamstrings are plucked bare,
her calf muscles and tendons
ready for the next pas de deux

The perfect arches of her feet:
these small harps.

ALICE

She's baking bread.
There's dough in her grey hair.
Her yellow apron's spotted
with kitchen years.
The bowl is white,
with a blue trim, chipped.

I'm hooked on the weave
of her biceps, her triceps,
the sinews that hold them in place.

Her strong arms. Her rooted grace.
All those loaves.

SAYING YES

I love to eat garlic
and nap on the lawn
in no particular order.
On the lawn in sunlight.
The sun on my back.

Now that's heaven,
I like to say, avoiding any
religious connection;
not at all like the holy folks
who used to linger at my door.

I used to ask them things like,
do you have any idea
where I can buy
knee socks
that don't fall down
or have you ever taken dancing lessons?

Or I would make an outrageous proposition,
asking, for instance,
would a young guy wearing
a black chenille bathrobe
(probably a ladies large)
in public, need gold chains
to be considered attractive?
And, if he asked you for a date,
after telling you that you were lovely,
would you say yes?

Heaven, I used to tell them
is just standing in line somewhere,
like VV Boutique, waiting for a poem.
Saying yes.

MARIE'S SECRET LOVER IS ELVIS

I want to imagine that Marie's big dream
was to go to Graceland,
like my friend the poet did one year
on the off chance he might see something
worthy of a poem.

He said the women, who were
mainly heavyweights, wore "I love Elvis" t-shirts,
"all glittered up", as he put it.
Their husbands kind of slid into the background,
their hair slick and sticky,
wearing white shirts rolled up at the biceps.

Everyone kind of moaned, he said,
when 'You ain't nothing but a hound dog' blasted out
and the gals grabbed their hubbies and hoofed it
into the night.

It was summer, he said,
and you could eat that Memphis air.

Since he was alone,
and after all, a poet,
when he saw Marie dancing in the street,
he went right up to her
and they started jiving, sweating
at Graceland, grace dripping everywhere,
like love.

EGGPLANT

I'm in the kitchen peeling
Japanese eggplant.
The end result is vaguely erotic.

This is a good thing, I tell myself,
because I've got to write
an erotic poem.

At the Superstore,
I always head for the eggplant first.
They are shiny purple,
fit nicely in the hand,
are easy to peel.

Suddenly, I think of a variation
of a Mae West line,
" is that an eggplant in your pocket
or are you just glad to see me?"

I'd like to try saying this
to some guy, at Value Village,
on a senior's Tuesday,
who might be looking

for an extra large shirt or
a radiator.
I try to imagine what would happen next.

Oh, forget it.
Although I seem to remember
one night in my youth
between palm trees and castanets,
on a beach somewhere.
Maybe, Greece.

Give me an eggplant to peel.
Any day. Delicious.

IF I LIVED IN TORONTO

I would go to the St. Lawrence Market
every Saturday and buy bread
the colour of beets and pumpkin.

I would grapple
with the choices between
purple and yellow broccoli.

I would straddle the apple stands
of Cox Orange Pippin, Gravenstein,
and the unnamed apple green as summer.

The peppers catch my eye;
they are golden, orange, red,
surrounded by Peruvian lutes.

I know that a sudden change in plans
leads to great fortune.
I buy them all.

I am broccoli. Beet bread,
I am apples. I am peppers.

MARGARET'S SHOES

I ask if I can take a picture of her shoes.
She says it's been a long day,
and poets are goofy as ever.

Well, maybe, I say,
but in the good old days,
when everyone thought poets were
backwater pond scum
and they knocked on each other's doors,
fell into fireplaces
and slept there,
weren't they pretty goofy too?

Be a plumber, she says,
it's nice and dark under the sink.
You can write there.

Poetry, she says,
is not toast.
Poets are not toaster repairmen. No.

Poets are goofy. They find shadows,
take pictures of shoes,
wear glitter.
Sing.

SOCKS

I know you never read reviews.
This is not a review.
This is a poem
about reading you a poem in Moose Jaw,
which means warm breeze.
This is a warm breeze of a poem.

You were wary.
Imagined I was either
an ex-girlfriend or a novelist with 800 pages
in an old Eaton's bag
I wanted you to read.

I was neither.

I noticed you wore no socks.
Decided to read you a poem about feet:
"the heart's navigators" I read.
You liked it.
Said I was just the kind of gal
who could have been
an ex-girlfriend in your salad days
when you wore socks,
were foolish,
read poems.

WHAT FEIGNS DEATH

blue beetles who roll on their backs,
legs stuck in the air or
my dog, who would roll on her back,
stop
breathing
as if there were an enemy
on the wind;
snakes, if you catch them
sunlit
will be still as rocks
until the shadow passes.
Or the guy walking
down the plum blossom street,
missing everything.

THE LIBRARY PLAZA

The piper in kilt and sporran,
ghillie broughes,
walks back and forth
in the library plaza.
It's spring's hottest night.
The sound is stately, ancient,
a lament that circles into us.

When he pauses,
I ask what he does in the daytime.
He says he's an oncologist.

Suddenly in the corner,
someone is doing the highland fling.
And suddenly, our hearts
are flinging for this lone piper,
the oncologist,
his lament filling up the night.

EASTER IN THE GARDEN

The cherry blossoms
fall on me as I weed the raspberry bed,
and I think I ought to write a poem
about the ravens making a ruckus
in the hemlock or
the warbler and the hummingbird
sharing a salmonberry branch.
All the birds are looking for dates;
even the solitary robin
I saw on the driveway this morning,
listening for worms.
I want to think
that the world is really like this:
the sun, the Gravenstein apple trees
in pink bloom.
But I know that grief
is never far away,
and someone in a café in Uruguay
will send me an email
saying she's there
because someone's died
halfway round the world.

The robin has found
his true love under the spruce.
The hummingbird is next in line.
Ah, the cherry blossoms fall.

WEDDING PICTURE

My mother wears my dreaming face,
two orchids, a hat and veil,
sensible shoes.

She is a sensible bride,
an orchid bride, blooming
in a small room.

Twenty relatives
arranged in layers behind her
bless this day
with their bright, hard names:
Feingold,
Opperman,
Glicksman,
Freeman,
Fischgrund.

I want to reach into the picture,
take her hand,
tell her life will never be
so perfectly arranged again.

Death will leave her sitting
alone in this small room
and the smiling ghosts will bless her,
will bless her.

THE PERFECT GUEST

You were always good with strangers;
could charm them
at the drop of a hat.

But not this stranger,
who has come uninvited to stay;
who won't watch the news,
or eat much,
who sleeps all day,
hardly moves.
A perfect guest.
Takes up so little space.
Can't remember anything,
except the shadows of ghosts
that drift in at night, singing.
This stranger, in daylight,
has no songs or dreams.
Will not be charmed.
Ever.

SUMMER

I'm in the back garden,
dead-heading fuchsias
at summer's end.
Around me are poppies
and the perfume of stargazer lilies.

I'm thinking of how this summer
of death has so quickly passed.
My friend's father,
dead suddenly at his desk.

Another friend's mother
with cancer of the pancreas,
stopped eating, died with grace.

My mother. And her slow dying.
Her mind gone,
she sleeps all day.
Imagines, when awake,
she's on a cruise ship.
Music and dancing
under the stars.
Stargazer lilies everywhere.
Perhaps she could waltz.
Not this summer.
Not this.
Summer.

TODAY, RAIN

No wind.
I do the ordinary:
make pickled cabbage;
freeze zucchini;
pick apples, beans,
Spanish lavender.
Read a week-old *Globe and Mail.*
Sleep. Without dreams.
Remember my friend who died
years ago in this season of rain.
When she left, her spirit spilled
into the room.

All day, the skies leaden,
I wait for the call.
The phone rings.
My brother says,
"Mom's gone."
Tells me he was in the room.
And her spirit? I ask.
Then grief rains down
among all the ordinary things.

GLOVES

I tell myself that just because
most of the maps in my head have returned,
it doesn't mean I know my way past grief.

When I find, in the pocket of her coat,
my mother's gloves:
fine, Italian burgundy leather,
still in the shape of her hands,
I remember her hands
and how the years twisted them
the way gardeners train the bonsai trees
into shapes that are trees/not trees.

I tell myself that the gloves that held
her bonsai hands are enough.
Suddenly, the streets blur again;
I strain to read the signs
and cannot find my way.

ALBUMS

They are already photographs

My grandfather wore plus fours.
My grandmother,
in white shoes, examining the roses.
The world was full of hats
and hatters,
garden paths,
bowlers. Everyone posed
in sunlight.
My father, the exception,
hatless and smiling,
a hat trick up his sleeve,
never mad as a hatter.
They rode in touring cars.
Posed with Indians.

The public lovers

She was always taller.
At the fraternity house party
she is centre stage, glowing,
a candle in black velvet,

silver shoes.
Her ankles are perfect. 1934.
In 1935, my father in tux and tie.
My mother in silk and pearls.
The next year she wears
an orchid on her wrist. Has a dance card.
Later, gardenias. Hatless.

And so they were caught dancing

Everything as they imagined.
Cheek to cheek. Ginger and Fred perfect.
She holds his hand.
A handkerchief between them.

My handkerchief parents in waiting.

Later, his letter

from the Philippine Village Hotel, 1977.
"Darling," and writes
of cocktails and shell collections,
boiled prawns and mangos,
pig knuckles,
of local notables

and pretty girls.
Lunch at the coconut plantation,
birding at the prison colony.
And a "lovely plump woman
who served up coffee, starfruit,
Spanish melon."(I am looking for a hat trick).
"Well, darling," he ends, "hope all is well at home."

They ride camels, elephants

The old elephant wears a sign,
"Rajastan Tourism". A camera finds them
hatless. Black and white.
A courtyard. My mother complained
of the food. Burning, she said.
The heat.
Darling, he said.
My black and white parents.

Later, in a desert
on a decorated camel.
My full colour invisible parents.

Her notes from Australia

Someone has a kidney stone.
The room is full of red dust.
Lunch, she complains, cold meat sandwiches.

Later, a real bed.
Fresh water pelicans.

She buys fresh water pearls.
A hat with feathers.

Tricked.
The photographs lost.

GHOSTS SPEAK

My mother's ghost

Of course I loved you.
We had 45 years together
before you died. Japan, wasn't it?
And you came home
in white porcelain. Ashes.
We had a rich life.
The orchids you grew.
The orchids I wore.

Once a woman came to the door.
It was winter.
She came right in.
Sat down. The children were there.
I offered her coffee didn't I?

I didn't think about it again.
Of course I loved you:
all your projects, your parks,
your beautiful suits, your fishing trips,
your trips away.
Your bad heart.

I kept busy.

My *father's ghost*

Of course I loved you.
You know how the world took me:
so much to do.
The business and the traveling,
the long fishing trips,
the parks I made.

You were my flower girl,
my rock solid girl.
My darling.
Our children.
I could never say how proud I was.
Never had the words.

But I remember you
on our wedding day:
with your cranberry hat
and lime veil
and all the orchids.

All the orchids.

GRANDMA, DANCING

When Grandma was sixty-five
she could touch her toes,
bending from the waist.
And dance, hairpins flying;
a gypsy under the burning moon.

Then she'd pour herself a sherry,
put her apron on,
make a steaming dish of chicken paprikash.

Grandma, I carry you in my apron pocket.
I make your lentil soup:
eggplant, apricots,
a little cinnamon to taste.

Grandma, I know your
steaming Hungarian ghost burns in me:
the cook,
the dancer, dancing,
bending from the waist.

GRANDPA

He knew something was coming.
It was 1912. Hungary. He knew
something was coming.
Heard the stories of pogroms, meaning
thunder, roar. The men forced
into town squares. Shot. The Jews burned
in the synagogues. Roaring.

My grandfather, that handsome
smart man, found someone
to teach him imperfect English
and wrote in exquisite imperfect script
to his Uncle Leo,
in South Bend, Indiana:
"I am 6'3" and wear a bowler hat.
So you will know me when I descend
on the train."

Because he knew something was coming,
better than fear and hate.
Because he allowed his life
and the lives of his daughters
and their children.
Because I am one of those.

BONE SCAN

She shows me my lumbar spine,
half my pelvis, hipbone. I am
bone solid, unholy, a skeleton
in black and white: discs, vertebrae
and joints, joined in her computer:
I am a nuclear medicine star.
I tell her it's the daily calcium for years,
the treadmill walks
watching the spine of the Strait,
its striations of tugboats, cruise ships,
fog, eagles, gulls.

I tell her it's my good genes,
and think of my mother's spine,
now ashes in an urn.
It's my mother's skeleton I carry;
my grandmother's and
her mother's and after that,
those other women with lost names
and my eyes.
Their good bones.

GREAT GRANDMOTHER

Nameless, I have her eyes.
Today, I find a shell in the rain,
purple as memory.
Dry, it fades to grey.
My great grandmother's eyes
catch the maples mad with spring,
the violets on the lawn, the long
shadows of swans on the harbour.

The rain's mirror:
my great grandmother's
Hungarian eyes.

If you say a prayer for the dead,
you say the name.

Her spring. The green of her heart
I never knew. Or the weeping.
Her lupine days,
the hats she wore.

And the summer hay fields,
something like God or love,
something easily named,
fading to grey.
The violets on the lawn,
swans on the harbour.

Or how she sang,
how she made soup,
how she loved,
how she died.

Did she plant carrots in the spring?
Cabbage?
Did she weave, did she dance? Did she dance?
Did she dream with my eyes?
What were the tides of her life?

The wash of it. The tides. The tides.
Broken shells.
Saying her name.

APPLES

You say Jonathan,
meaning your son who died.
And I think of apples
in the October orchard:
the bright shine of them
as they fall.
Cancer you say.

And his brother,
laying on the couch,
his skin bronzed,
his adrenals gone
from the sorrow.

It's these words that string
the warp of your pain.

You're a man who walks fast;
you never miss a thing.
Not even death,
that old apple seller
wearing a broken cloak.
Not even him.

TIGGY

We called all day for you:
in the woods, by the pond,
under the bamboo.
The next morning
we found you in the wind,
brought you in,
cushioned you with foam, towels.
You didn't move.
Death was already on you.

Oh, you scratcher of posts,
you beautiful stretcher,
you skywatcher,
you apple tree acrobat,
you nap companion,
you dream cat,
you dancer.
Go.

YVONNE

It is a blue heron day, a geese
and gull day.
Tide out. Sunlight. May.
Mock orange everywhere.
Everyone's out: plugged-in runners,
old ladies with small,
perfect dogs, young mothers
dazed and strolling. And I think of you,
your child bonding with tubes
in intensive care.
Your world divided into envelopes
of worry, watching, half sleep.
You already know
what is the worst thing,
the second worst,
and down the line.
You're already making bargains
with anything:
the lamppost, the devil,
the terrible apple trees,
ghosts. Anything
you can name.

I'M THINKING OF ALL THE THINGS THAT BLOOM IN THE WORLD

like lewisia, with white cactus- like flowers;
or libertia, of the iris family from Chile;
lomatia, a shrub from Australia;
luculia, a shrub from the Himalayas;
or lunaria, called honesty, whose seeds
are wrapped in small moons;
then, leukemia, that blooms
with small white flowers in the blood.

Your leukemia.
And while it bloomed, you learned
to breathe, tried everything, even
the oncologist's bouquet.

You grew a garden of small moons
on your balcony, watched them bloom
red. Watched them bloom
life.

ORANGES

We're eating tofu with black bean sauce,
prawns with garlic at the Noodle House.
You tell me how you nearly died,
one January morning:
an aortal tear at 11 a.m.
and suddenly, nearly dead, bleeding,
filled with morphine,
you chanted "No" in the ambulance,
all the way Calgary.
You tell me, between courses,
how they split you open, sternum to navel,
packed you with ice cubes.
And I begin to imagine ice cubes
in the shape of stars, starfish, small brilliant hearts,
ice flowers.
I stop, mid-imagining.
ask to see your scar.
You pull down the neck of your Stanfield,
show me.

For two weeks, you tell me,
your life was morphine dreams,
like the afterimage on the tv: you see
an old woman in a dark room who sells belts
and buttons. She shows you a gilded box
filled with eggs. Then, you're on
an abandoned carousel in the rain.

When you wake your mind moves underwater.
When the doctors tell you
about deep hypothermic circulatory arrest,
you see cops and robbers,
think oceans, heat. Words scramble.
You call an orange an antelope,
call an avocado a raven.

Finally one autumn day smelling of ice, flowers,
you eat an orange. Call it that.
Rejoice.

KATHLEEN'S HAT

For Kathleen Ryan

Kathleen died at Equinox
after the bright summer
she learned how to die.

She sat, facing the Strait,
the smell of seaweed and roses
on the wind.
Her face, a pale rose,
turned to the sun.
She watched the gulls
circle and glide.

"This is it, honey, the real thing,"
she said.

She leaned into me,
for heat, for life,
I held her hand, read old poems,
told jokes, juggled words,
while the roses of cancer bloomed in her.

I still want to call her up,
tell her secrets,
bring her Stargazer lilies
and Gravenstein apples.

I wear Kathleen's sensible straw hat
and think of her, think of her
blooming at Equinox.

DANGEROUS FOOD

On the evening news I watch the reporter,
a man of large heart, named Sorious,
sweep and wash the floors
of the AIDS hospital in Zambia.
One man, a skeleton who smiles,
tells him of his three women, five children,
all dead.
There is blood on the floor.
Tears.

I watch the next night;
know this is dangerous food.
I am already poisoned.

I can say sorrow,
I can say suffering.
I can write a cheque.
And then, for instance,
go to the garden, pick chard,
sorrel, carrots, thyme,
make soup.

Or take mustard greens gone to flower
to my neighbour, for his chickens,
in trade for eggs.
Talk about the rain.

I move easily
into the elsewhere of the everyday:
the lists of things undone;
the floors to sweep and wash;
the bread rising in the clean kitchen.
The winter sun shining,
everywhere.

WALKING TOWARD HOPE: FLEEING SUDAN

They walk toward hope
as if it were a place.
The donkeys move through the desert.
There are no signposts.
Behind them, the goats.
The heat hangs on them
and the family that walks beside them.

They walk into the heat
which is colder than the fear
they leave behind.

It's 45 degrees Celsius.
Heat rises from their backs
as if it were a map.

IF I HAD ADAM'S HAND

for Adam, tailor, waiting in the refugee camp in Chad

it would be still as glass;
it would know how to hold onto the smile of a stranger
as if it were food;
it would know how to dig for water in the desert;
it would know how to sew and shape cloth;
it would know how to wash blood
from the body of his son;
it would know how to make a tent
in the terrible camps of Chad;
it would know how to wait;
it would shine.

TAKE FOR INSTANCE

The elephants of Banda Ache
named Rachmat, Medang, Ida,
who on any other day
would have tourists on their backs
for the slow walk through the jungle.
Take for instance,
their slow heartbeats,
their hearts the size of cellos.

Take for instance
how they stood in the palm shade of the village
that morning listening
to the earth move before it moved,
and crying, ran into the hills
before the wave broke
Banda Ache.

Take for instance
how they came back to the ruined village,
moved concrete and rooftops, broken trees;
lifted the dead with their trunks.

Take for instance
how they heard in their cello hearts
the new ghosts sing to them.

EXPLAINING RAIN

I have come to talk of rain
to the girl who moves sand
from the courtyards.
She is there not for the love of sand,
or the way her days move
through the heat.
No.

She is a girl dressed
in the ribbons of death:
her mother, father, aunt, cousins,
dead with the wasting.
She feeds her sisters,
her small brother, whose wounds
never heal.

In the dark morning
she comes, before the desert birds,
with a small blue plastic pan
to move the sand:
each grain that will return
again and again.

I stand by her
in the red heat,
say rain,
say call it tears.
She knows tears.

I say, call it water.
She knows water,
carries it on her head
from the well, two miles away.

I say, like trees,
like shade,
kneel in the sand
to draw hemlock, fir, maple,
draw the shape of trees, leaves.

I say how rain
comes in winter like slow waves.
I draw waves.

She is silent,
she turns to me,
bends again,
says rain.

NO MAN CAN CROSS THE SAME RIVER TWICE BECAUSE NEITHER MAN NOR RIVER ARE THE SAME

for Julie Holder

Because Phoebe, your black dog
sleeps in your office,

because sometimes she leaps
into your arms,

because you know black dogs
and black sticks,

because you love Thai silk
and dream of Africa,

because once you waited
for the late postman,

because the news might be bad
and was,

because you are the queen of worry
and necklaces,

because you are my quiet sister,
who never crosses the same river twice.

SNOWDROPS

You're standing by the piano
at the Royal York.
All around you: music, guys in suits.
You're wearing a black leather jacket
and Thursday's long meeting.
We walk to the Kit Kat,
order agnolotti with pesto, curried soup.
The talk turns to snowdrops;
the ones you took from an abandoned house
one spring, for your last garden, where you grew
the exotic: edamame soybeans, Japanese squash,
mizuna, arugula.

Now, you tell me, you only have room
for basil in a box. Instead,
you grow children with beautiful names:
Tessa and Quinn.
And in one corner of this ordinary garden,
you plant love, plant memory, plant snowdrops.
Watch them grow.

IF I WERE TO SEND YOU A GIFT

I would find a box.
In it I'd place the white skull
of a seabird,
a clam shell decorated
with a staccato of barnacles.

For your daughters,
two stone hearts
carved in Ghana.

I would send you a friend's book,
which is a long poem
about the heart
and what turns it to stone,
what breaks it.

I'd send you a Doisineau photograph
of children in a ruined car,
in a ruined landscape.
France, 1944, joy falling from them.
A gift.

SECRETS

When I see you,
you're trailing the earpiece
of your cell phone;
leather cases spill around you
like small mountains.
You look like the courier guy.
You sit close,
on the edge of the glass table;
tell me of your frenzied life,
the art that centres you,
the light and burnished sky,
your daughter's poems,
secrets on the back of everything.

DAVID'S TREES

You show me the perfect drawing
of a broken tree branch
still blooming,
you drew last spring;
then the Sudek photographs of cherry trees.
Later, your collection: framed splinters
from a Zeppelin;
a piece of Winchester Cathedral,
from 1079;
an Inuit snow scraper;
your daughters' paintings;
a box filled with the small bones
of birds and blue stones.

Nearby, your luminous wife
plays Teleman on the Steinway,
wearing her best sadness and blue shoes.

Later, she'll decorate
a cake for your birthday,
play for you.
And for a while,
your world will be perfect:
a tree branch blooming in June,
white blossoms falling everywhere
like love.

NEARLY FATHER'S DAY

I'm hanging the laundry,
listening to the robins and wrens
singing in the salmonberry.

I'm not thinking of my father,
whose heart blew up in his 68th year. No.
I notice that it's nearly summer,
see it in the shadows of the apple trees.
Then I learn that your father has just died.

I want to say that I know the consequence
of grief: the lost keys,
the sentences half finished
while the mind finds
the shape of its own sorrow.

But you already know this sadness
is constant as summer.
And the birds, who know everything,
keep singing.

I HOLD THE PHOTOGRAPH

of your father
wearing a beautiful silk tie.
Who was this man
with such kind eyes?
This man who loved small things:
carved wooden heads
from the Bering Sea;
stone ravens;
steam engines in bell jars;
Chinese snuff bottles carved
from coral, ivory, amethyst, stone.

I imagine him holding
a carved Egyptian frog,
green in his hand,
in clear wonder,
in still grace.

KEITH AND HIS SEASONS

Some guy calls this morning,
wants to know if the Horsefly Bridge
is passable. I tell him
I can't help. I'm not in Horsefly,
although I've been there once in spring.
I tell him to use Google Earth,
which you showed me one winter day;
passing over Scotland like an eagle,
where you were born.

You're a man who carves stone;
imagines ravens and bears,
turns them into smooth and shining poems.

You're a man who offers his arm
to any lady who needs it, including me,
one rainy fall night, if I recall.

You're a man of the seasons,
who sounds like Sean Connery,
in summer; only better.
Who can resist you?

I COULD SAY

bilateral investment treaties,
NAFTA, WTO,
Globalization and the North,
meaning Noel;
the tall guy in jeans and leather,
the quiet, kind one
who loves Elizabeth,
plays Bach on the guitar,
cooks, juggles longevity.

I could say Noel,
who tells me how he once
lay on the bathroom tiles
after too much Glenlivet,
said he'd studied the floor for hours,
saw bilateral patterns.

I could say, Noel,
watch the sky.
There is a raven there with tattered wings.
He owns everything;
trades his song for the currency
of joy.
Invest in him.

IT'S TOO LATE FOR A WHITE DRESS, CAMILLA

Wear red silk, the colour of blood
and sunsets;
the colour of heartbreak and roses.
Carry Iceland poppies.
Watch their small petals fall like love.
When a thousand cameras flash,
hold the bare stems high.
Smile. Say wife.

WINTER PLANTING

First, you fill the wheelbarrow
with last year's compost
where the memory of orange rinds
and apple cores is just that.

You move to the iris
that stopped blooming last summer
and lift a hundred blubs
that used to be thirty.

Then you dig, find something shining:
the gold wedding ring you'd given up for lost
years before. Your great aunt's, dated 1898,
engraved, " from Leo to Salie."
You stop, surrounded by the iris that stopped
blooming and think of your marriages that never bloomed:
those old sorrows that got put under the sink in a bucket.

You fill up the iris bed,
one slow shovelful at a time,
and with your left hand, reach deep
into the cold February earth
and replant the ring.
Forever.

IN THIS SMALL ROOM WITH LILACS: ESL on Linden Street

I've arrived to read them poems.
I explain the word pomegranate:
say: red, round, sweet, rubies,
and they smile, nod.
Yes, says Ludmilla,
in the Ukraine, the same.
Osmany, from Cuba says,
sometime we have them at Christmas.
Yes, he says, rubies.

I move on to starfish,
show them the ones on my bracelet.
Say how they cling to rocks at low tide,
in a magenta wash.
Soo Jin says, in Korea, they are
sometimes the colour of the sun.

Then red-winged blackbirds.
I show them a picture;
tell them how I hear their song
like falling water, when I shower outside
each morning.

Outside, even in winter? asks Alexandra,
imagining Russian ice and snowdrift.
Even in winter, I say.

But this spring, there are ravens,
hummingbirds,
the music of blackbirds,
that I hear every morning,
speaking a language
I can't understand.

FOR THE PLANET

A girl is alone on the stage.
She is on the sill of her life.
She is on the sill of the planet.
If she could, she would be a forest.

She is on the sill of her life.
She would be balsam, pine, hemlock, fir.
If she could, she would be a forest.
She would be eucalyptus.

She would be balsam, pine, hemlock, fir.
She would exhale oxygen.
She would be eucalyptus.
She is speaking French. It is not her language.

She would exhale oxygen.
"Tu pense que tu voles comme un oiseau."
She is speaking French. It is not her language.
She is speaking in treesong, birdcall.
"Tu pense que tu voles comme un oiseau."
She is on the sill of the planet.
She is speaking in treesong, birdcall.
A girl is alone on the stage.

IN YOUR HOUSE

is a kind of stillness:
a quiet that doesn't mean
no one is speaking.
The other stillness of the heart.
On your mantle:
an iridescent hen,
a vase filled with buttons,
a carved rooster with spats.
I want them all.
Outside, the crows swing by,
slick and insistent.
Inside we drink lemon grass tea,
speak of poems, poets,
exaltations, apples,
buttons.

THOSE OLD POEMS

are like the wooden boat on the beach
I saw once, the waves
hitting it over and over, the barnacles already
at it. A few misguided starfish clinging
to the sides. Mussels.
Something beautiful still left.
Tide in, tide out.

ACKNOWLEDGEMENTS

Some of these poems have appeared in chapbooks published by Leaf Press: *Anecdote* and *Witch in White*. Some were broadcast on the CBC. They have also been published on line on the website the University of Toronto kindly set up for me, http://www.library.utoronto.ca/canpoetry/morton

These poems own much to the encouragement and help of my companion, Rod Punnett, and to the inspired guidance of Patrick Lane, at whose poetry retreats many of these poems were written.

I'd like to thank WestJet Airlines, for all my years as poet of the skies and all the passengers for whom I wrote poems. As well, I'd like to thank Daimler-Chrysler for providing me with a PT Cruiser into my first forays into the lovely world of Random Acts of Poetry. I'd like to thank the Fairmont Hotels, who allow me luxurious accommodations when I travel for poetry, and Fujifilm, who have given me a superb F10 digital camera. Prairie Naturals Vitamins has not only provided me with their products that keep me healthy, but purchases my books for my own Random Acts of Poetry at various literary events across Canada. And abebooks, the world's largest online bookseller, deserves special thanks for now being my personal sponsor, as well as supporting the National Random Acts of Poetry Week for two years. I would also like to thank The Canada Council for the Arts for their support of National Random Acts of Poetry week, as well as The Victoria READ Society for their enthusiasm for this project.

Finally, I want to thank the following: my kind-hearted publisher, Marty Gervais; my editor, Susan Stenson, whose suggestions I nearly always follow; Charles Mountford, whose line "Marie's secret lover was Elvis", I borrowed from his poem "Secret Lover", from his book of poetry, *The Night the Ducks Got Loose* and for suggesting the title of this book. Lastly, I thank all my poetry friends at Planet Earth Poetry who have heard most of these poems read and applauded them, much to my delight.

MARQUIS
MEMBER OF SCABRINI GROUP
Québec, Canada
2007